Affluent Client, Customer & Patient Attraction
for NYC Businesses

Affluent Client, Customer & Patient Attraction
for NYC Businesses

5 WAYS TO TRANSFORM YOUR NYC BUSINESS TO
MAGNETICALLY ATTRACT CLIENTS, CUSTOMERS OR
PATIENTS WHO WILL EAGERLY PAY YOU MORE...

by

Chris Sewell

www.ChrisSewellDigitalMedia.nyc

DISCLAIMER

The author has made every attempt to be as accurate and complete as possible in the creation of this publication/PDF, however he / she does not warrant or represent at any time that the contents within are accurate due to the rapidly changing nature of the Internet. The author assumes no responsibility for errors, omissions, or contrary interpretation of the subject matter herein. Any perceived slights of specific persons, peoples, or organizations other published materials are unintentional and used solely for educational purposes only.

This information is not intended for use as a source of legal, business, accounting or financial advice. All readers are advised **to seek services of competent professionals in legal, business, accounting, and finance field.** No representation is made or implied that the reader will do as well from using the suggested techniques, strategies, methods, systems, or ideas; rather it is presented for news value only.

The author does not assume any responsibility or liability **whatsoever** for what you choose to do with this information. Use your own judgment. Consult appropriate professionals before starting a business. Any perceived remark, comment or use of organizations, people mentioned and any resemblance to characters living, dead or otherwise, real or fictitious does not mean that they support this content in any way.

There are no guarantees of income made, traffic delivered or other promises of any kind. Readers are cautioned to reply on their own judgment about their individual circumstances to act accordingly. By reading any document, the reader agrees that under no circumstances is the author responsible for any losses, direct or indirect, that are incurred as a result of use of the information contained within this document, including - but not limited to errors, omissions, or inaccuracies.

Published by Chris Sewell Digital Media
www.ChrisSewellDigitalMedia.nyc

Printed by CreateSpace
Printed in the United States of America

ISBN-13: 978-1522909224
ISBN-10: 1522909222

Table of Contents

Table of Contents

HOW TO USE THIS REPORT TO
TRANSFORM
YOUR NYC BUSINESS IN THIS

New Economy

In NYC, competition is forcing you to lower your prices...and that stinks! You're not charging customers, clients or patients as much as you want, _which isn't fair to you._

Thanks to the Internet, **the New Economy gives potential customers, clients, and patients in NYC more power now than ever before**. Prices for what you charge are very transparent online.

Comparison shopping sites like Groupon and Living Social offer deals for what you sell that often force you to lower your prices. And if you've used these services to find new business, you quickly see that you're dealing with lower-quality customers, clients or patients who never buy from you again...unless you offer than another 50% off deal.

Your online reputation in Yelp, Merchant Circle and other online directories can tarnish your business without you knowing it.

The Internet has made it very easy for newcomers to take business away from you. If you don't know how to use the various online advertising sources, and you're still using the Yellow Pages and newspapers to find business, you may even see your profits dropping.

There is a better way and in this guide I'll show you exactly how I've helped NYC business owners transform "WHO" they sell to so they no longer need to compete on price.

FIERCE COMPETITION HITS YOU FROM MANY ANGLES

In this New Economy, the Internet is where people research a business and decide whether or not to contact you or your nearest competitor.

How you handle that first contact and subsequent followup, determines whether you get the new business or not. You must have a system in place to reconnect with every email, phone and website form lead that hits your office.

You want this system to be as automated as possible so you can focus on servicing the needs of current customers, clients or patients.

There are very few barriers for others to enter your field. The knowledge to start a business in your field is readily available to anyone online, unless you're in the medical, legal or financial field which requires specialized education and licensing.

As I write this, NYC is undergoing a major transformation itself. In my Clinton Hill, Brooklyn neighborhood, scafolds line every other block. It seems that every inch of the city is being renovated. Money is pouring into the city from all directions.

The question is how your business can get more of it. This is what I want to show you in this guide.

COMPETING ON PRICE IS THE WEAKEST MARKETING STRATEGY--ESPECIALLY IN NYC WHEN THERE'S SO MANY PEOPLE EAGER TO PAY YOU MORE

In 2005, I read a book called "Blue Ocean Strategy" by W. Chan Kim & Renee Mauborgne. The premise of the book was that businesses should go where the profits and growth as and the competition isn't. In New York City's overcrowded industries, competing on price alone results in a bloody "red ocean" - a true race to the bottom.

After reading this book, I began to put together a strategy to help business owners avoid the "red ocean" and transform their businesses into "blue ocean" enterprises.

To do this you need two things:

- A sophisticated followup system to reconnect with all leads that enter your sales funnel.

- A system to target people who have money to spend on what you sell - affluent customers, clients and patients.

The bulk of this guide focuses on these two items. Should you decide to use the strategies I reveal in this guide, you most transform the way you market for more customers, clients and patients.

The Yellow Pages will not help you. Neither will billboard signs, radio, or newspaper ads. That's not how the affluent search for products and services anymore.

Contecting with the affluent in NYC requires a mix of Internet and direct mail marketing in this New Economy. This has nothing to do with SEO or ranking your website in Google.

COUPON SITES LIKE GROUPON AND LIVING SOCIAL ONLY BRING "BARGAIN-HUNTERS" TO YOUR DOORS

If you check out coupon sites like **Groupon** and **Living Social**, you'll find numerous products and services at deep discounts. These sites are a bargain hunters dream come true. This is not where you want to find new business.

How can you compete? Each year you lower prices to keep your income stable, while working longer hours. Does this make you angry? **It should.**

The Internet gives NYC businesses like yours a ton of competition. The New Economy also means it's more important to differentiate yourself from your competitors.

As a result of the 2007 Great Recession, many businesses that catered to the *"general-masses"* got smart. They added a

high-end component to their business model to make themselves **recession-proof.**

REBRAND YOUR BUSINESS TO STAY AHEAD OF YOUR COMPETITION

Take for example, **Hallmark Gold Crown**. You've no doubt purchased greeting cards from this well known store chain. In 2004, Hallmark operated 4,000 stores, targeting the "general masses" who are typically bargain hunters.

Hallmark *rebranded itself* as HMK to provide gifts and cards to affluent customers. Their new stores have a more luxurious look and feel than their old Hallmark Gold Crown stores.

I know this is only one example. I don't want to load this book up with a million more examples. You might get bored.

Companies that completely rely on the "general-masses" to grow their business, will be forever controlled by the ups and downs of the economy. This is because, the "general-masses" are controlled by the ups and downs of the economy. Hallmark is transforming its business. **You should transform yours too.**

Many jobs that employed the "general-masses" will never return. If your retail store, firm or practice is focused on attracting the "average" NYC resident, you'll find that they are very price-sensitive.

This is why you want to transform your business to attract affluent NYC residents who are highly skilled workers or business owners, where price isn't their main concern.

CHANGE YOUR CUSTOMERS, CLIENT & PATIENTS FROM THE "MASSES" TO THE "AFFLUENT"

Stop trying to compete for dollars at the low end when the upper-end is eager to pay you more. You won't win. **Move your business or practice to a new model** and you'll win those affluent NYC residents.

Transform your business into a model that caters to people who rarely look for the lowest price when they shop or need professional services. You want people who are more concerned with the experience and knowledge you offer.

But, more importantly, you want customers who'll pay you a premium for your ability to clear the confusion in their heads about what products and services are best for them.

If you want to join the ranks of the *'Super-Elite, Recession-Proof'* NYC businesses, you must go where the money is and plant your flag now. There are far too many business owners in NYC willing to cater to the general-masses and compete with coupon sites that offer very low prices.

You shouldn't be one of them.

If you already have affluent customers, it's time you got more of them. I must admit, the work to attract affluent customers is greater than what's required to attract the "general masses".

Prospecting the "general-masses" is low-hanging fruit.

I FELL VICTIM TO THAT SAME THINKING DURING THE EARLY YEARS OF MY LEAD-

GENERATING, MARKETING CONSULTING PRACTICE.

Back in 2000, I focused on the small business owner and the part-time business owner who wanted to grow. It took me about 5 years before I realized I was doing it all wrong.

When I started implementing affluent client attraction secrets revealed by **Dan Kennedy, Pam Danziger, William Danko, and Mark Penn,** I realized there was a niche to every niche.

Every niche has 90% who don't have much money and 10% with a bunch of money. Every niche has this dynamic. I challenge you to name any niche that doesn't. When you market your practice to affluent people, your business will have less competition because your competitors will target people on the lower economic end of the ladder.

YOU MUST UNDERSTAND WHO THESE AFFLUENT PEOPLE ARE

Your approach to attracting affluent customers, clients or patients must be **very different** than your approach to attracting the "general-masses".

The affluent hangout in different places...they read different publications...they have different fears...their concerns are more complex. I'll point you in the right direction to hook them and reel them in one fish at a time.

The extra work you must put into transforming your business to attract the affluent is not bigger than the opportunity in front of you. It's not 10x more difficult to attract a high-paying customer than a discount seeking one.

...you just have to understand how to do it.

You must be a little smarter...a little more systematic...and a little more targeted in your approach.

I'll show you how to do all of this in this guide. You just need to put my techniques into action. Targeting the **right** affluent prospects will be critical to your success. I will discuss this in detail.

THE MEDIA HAS YOU THINKING THAT... AFFLUENT CUSTOMERS, CLIENTS OR PATIENTS ARE HARD TO FIND ...IGNORE THAT STUFF

If you listen to the media, whenever there's a market downturn, you would think everyone is pinching pennies and cutting up their credit cards.

If you focus on the news, you might think that affluent people are hurting financially too. You might also believe your practice is doomed to take a downturn whenever the economy falters, because all of your customers are taking a financial hit.

If your business caters to people with networths under $500K, you would be correct. Your business will suffer when the economy craters.

Running a business that caters to people who have a networth under $500K means you own a business that is controlled by the economy.

ALL IS NOT LOST... YOU CAN REINVENT YOUR BUSINESS...

AND IF YOU KEEP READING, I'LL SHOW YOU HOW

Despite the challenges you face in your industry, some NYC businesses have transformed their models by attracting more affluent customers than they can handle. These owners are enjoying more free time, while earning more yearly income.

No matter where your business is located in NYC and no matter what condition it's in, **You can attract more affluent customers than you can handle.**

This "special class" of customer wants to pay you higher prices, even if you charge more than your competitors. Just follow the little-known, but effective techniques I'll reveal to you in this guide.

New Opportunity

TO FINALLY DISTANCE YOURSELF FROM YOUR COMPETITION...AND REBRAND YOUR NYC BUSINESS

According to Spectrem Group Research (http://spectrem.com) the fastest growing demographic is the "mass-affluent", households with a networth of $500K to $1MM.

These people are the "special class" of customer, client or patient you should start targeting in NYC. NYC has plenty of people in this group. If you business was in Alabama or Kansas, this would not be the case.

But in NYC, you have it easy.

Affluent people are all around you and they have money to spend. This wasn't always the case in NYC. If you remember New York of the 70s, wealth was leaving the city. There was a large gap bewteen the wealthy and the poor.

There wasn't much of a wealthy middle like what there is now. These wealthy people don't all live on the Upper West Side of Manhattan.

Many live in renovated brownstones in Williamsburg, Fort Greene and Park Slope in Brooklyn. They live in nice homes in Queens and the Bronx. They want to buy from you and are willing to travel a little further out to be your next customer, client or patient.

You just need to learn how to reach them and I'll show you how.

DESPITE THE INCREASED DEMAND FOR WHAT YOU DO IN NYC, YOUR PRICES ARE FLAT -- BECAUSE YOU'RE TARGETING THE WRONG TYPE OF PERSON

This might not be the case so much if you're in a housing related industry in NYC. Real estate is booming everywhere in the city. Scafolds flying high in just about every neighborhood, except East New York, Brooklyn & Fordham, Bronx, sadly.

If your marketing is targeted towards anyone who wants your product or services, you're making a big mistake. You need to start targeting a special class of buyer. I'm talking about the "mass-affluent".

Who are the "mass-affluent"?

They're the people that moved out of the "middle-class" to a place a few economic steps upwards. The media likes to talk about the "disappearing" middle class. As if some space ship sucked them off the earth.

Here's what happened to the old middle class...

One-third moved down the economic ladder because their skills became obsolete.

The factory worker, the assembly line manager, the guy who worked with his hands to feed his famil, replaced by either automation or the Chinese factory that produces quicker results at a lower price. The other two-thirds of the old middle-class moved up the economic ladder.

They embraced the Internet and started online businesses. They used the Internet to research how to start a business or improve their traditional business. They learned to outsource certain tasks to be competitive with larger companies.

These two-thirds are what's called the **"mass-affluent."** These are the types of people you should target, because they're far less likely to shop for discounts.

They might want a toothbrush at a discount...but when it comes to certain products and services: Beauty, Home Repairs, Legal, Financial, or Medical -- they want to be treated like celebrities.

And, they're willing to pay you that celebrity price.

The second group that you should target is the **"affluent."**

They have a networth of $1MM to $3MM, according to Wealth Engine (http://www.wealthengine.com). These two groups of affluent people can truly transform your NYC business.

WHO ARE THESE PEOPLE WILLING TO PAY YOU HIGHER PRICES & FEES?

Many of the "mass-affluent" work high-paying jobs because they have specialized skills.   They're middle to upper level managers at technology, medical, and financial firms, as well as staffing agencies. In NYC, we have more of these business owner types than another state in America.

If you want more free time outside the office and you also want to earn more income, **fill your pipeline with affluent prospects.**

The good news for you is there are **13.5MM households** with a networth between $500K and $1MM, according to *US Census* data. Many live in NYC & NJ, or are willing to drive across state lines to reach you, if you truly differentiate yourself from a local competitor.

This class of affluent looks pretty normal.

They look and talk just like you and most shop where you shop each day. Read the *'Millionaire Next Door'*, by William Danko if you want an in-depth education on their norms.

Let me give you more facts about the mass-affluent discussed in *U.S. Federal Reserve* studies, the *'Millionaire Next Door'*, and *US Census Data*.

The Mass-Affluent

This demographical pool is the fastest growing in the world right now and many live here in NYC around you and me.

As more people embrace the Internet to learn how to create wealth and deepen their education on a wide variety of topics -- there'll be more mass-affluent prospects for what you sell than you can handle.

Here's what you need to know about them.

- They have a networth from $500,000 to $1MM.

- There are 21.6 million such households nationwide according to **Pam Danziger** of **Unity Marketing**. (US Census data claims 13.5MM households). Many live in NYC.

- Most of their networth is tied up in retirement accounts.

- They read publications by **Suze Orman** and **Money** magazine to learn how to make smart decisions with their money.

- 60% of the women in these two-person households are involved in all investment decisions. *(Don't make the mistake of thinking that the men make all money decisions.)*

- They are typically a two-person salaried household that each earns $100,000 to $250,000 yearly.

- They used to be in the traditional middle-class group, but they've upgraded their skills

- They include small business owners that learned how to start or grow their business from resources found online. *(This also includes blue- and white- collar workers with specialized skills.)*

- They shop at Saks, Bloomingdales, and Nordstroms to splurge a little, but also loves to shop at Target and Wal-Mart.

- This group aspires to be affluent, but values staying within their budget.

- They are highly educated. They attended major universities and received advanced degrees.

The Affluent

Then you have the affluent patient-prospect. These are people with a networth of $1MM to $3MM. This group has the largest discretionary income than any generation before them. This new breed of affluent is spending their wealth, especially on anti-aging and weight loss services.

- They have a networth from $1MM to $MM. Age 35-55.

- There are 7.5 million such households nationwide according to **Pam Danziger** of **Unity Marketin.** Many live in NYC.

- Over the last 2 decades this group has exploded with in wealth.

- The flattening of the globe has spawned more of these millionaires all over the world.

- Many live in middle-class neighborhoods. Some live next door to you and me in NYC. The "shadow" millionaire according to **William Danko** in **'The Millionaire Next Door'.**

- They shop at Saks, Bloomingdales, and Nordstroms to splurge, but also not ashamed to shop at Target and Wal-Mart to blend into the middle-class scene.

- They read The Wall Street Journal and Forbes. Personally, I prefer Investor's Business Daily.

- They may own a second, small home outside their primary state. In NYC, this group may own a second home in Long Island or Upstate NY which they use on the weekends to get away from the city.

- They follow political and world events, and lean Conservative.

SUPER SWEET SPOT FOR HIGH-PAYING CUSTOMERS, CLIENTS, AND PATIENTS WHO WILL RETURN MULTIPLE TIMES

If you really want to focus like a laser beam on the best customers to totally transform your business or practice -- focus on two classes of people: **Women Over 40 and Men Over 50.**

These two groups will fill your pipeline with more business than you can handle. They have the money and are willing to pay a bit more for expertise and a unique experience.

I'll go more in-depth on the best ways to approach these two groups later in this book. There are more than enough affluent prospects in NYC to help you build a recession-proof business.

When I started targeting affluent clients for my lead-generation, marketing consulting practice -- I enjoyed more income with fewer clients and less stress.

It also allowed me to better focus on my clients...connect with them more emotionally...and get referrals without asking for them. That's what attracting affluent customers, clients of patients can do for one's business.

If you don't ignore them they will be loyal. Do you like being ignored? No one likes being ignored. The affluent are more likely to get repeat services from you, just as long as, you don't screw things up and ignore them once you get them.

When you sell your products or services, you should outline a list of other products or services to offer them based on the last product or service purchased.

Ritz Carlton customers *(affluent)* are more loyal than Holiday Inn customers *(general masses)*. A Holiday Inn customer is looking for the cheapest room to lay his head. Red Roof, Quality Inn, Best Western -- it doesn't matter to him as long as he gets the lowest price.

> Monthly newsletters *(snail mail, not email)*...makes it easy to stay in contact with prospects about what you can do for them.

When you deal with Ritz Carlton type customer, they will not accept being ignored. They expect a newsletter, video seminar, or special event to hold their attention. This allows you to get more of their money.

Let's take the face for example...

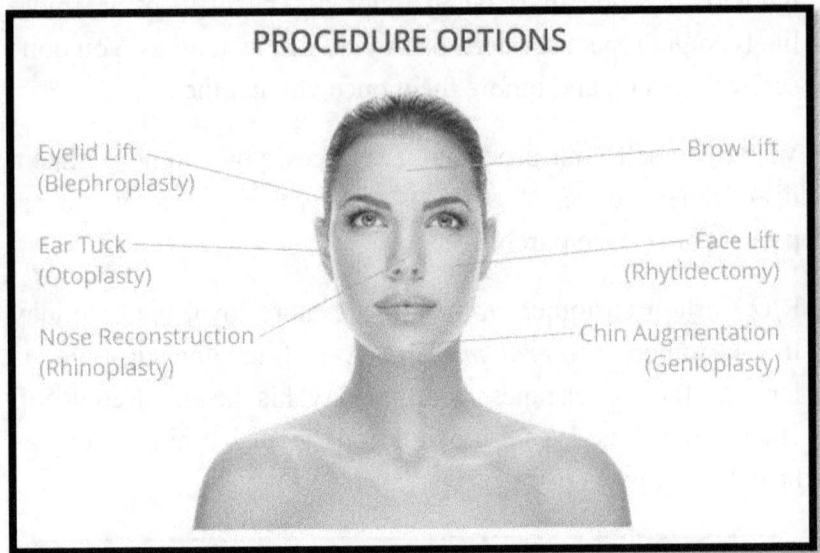

If a patient gets a Rhinoplasty or a laser facial resurface, after they heal, you should offer them maybe an eyelid lift...ear tuck...brow lift...or Genioplasty. Don't wait for them to contact you about what service they should get next. Take a proactive approach and tell them what they should get next.

People who price shop *(the general masses),* will use whatever service offers them the biggest coupon discount. It's time for you to reinvent your business and target affluent people who are concerned with quality, not price.

They're a Better Source Of Referrals

Birds of a feather, flock together. Millionaires tend to surround themselves with other millionaires. Men and women who buy what you sell ofetn hang around other men and women who want the same types of prosucts and services.

When your affluent customer tells their millionaire friends about the positive experience with your business or practice -- **it's easy to get referrals.** If you do a great job with them, their affluent friends will know. If you make a mess of things and ignore them, they'll know about that too and ***avoid you like you had a the plague.***

Imagine what your business would look like if you were to take advantage of the opportunity in front of you today. Imagine putting a system in place that attracts affluent customers, clients or patients to your like a magnet. You could work less hours, manage fewer client or patients, and spend more fun time with family. You can do all of this while making more money.

That's exactly what happened to *Dr. Giri Singh, Surgeon at Rosedale Ivy Surgery*. He implemented the 5 New Economy techniques that I teach in this resource to transform his medical practice and attract affluent patients.

Another medical professional who is working less and making more is *Dr. Dan Sinhoff, of the Sinhoff Medical Spa & Weight Loss clinic.* Dan repositioned his practice targeting men over 50 and women over 40, with a networth of at least $500K.

What would your medical practice look like if you acquired more affluent patients who want to pay you twice what you currently charge? **Now, imagine that happening within the next 12 months.**

Here are five ways you can start doing it immediately.

Reinvent Your Business

With These 5 New Economy Ways To Attract Affluent Customers, Clients, or Patients Who Will Pay You More

New Economy Rule #1:
Develop your personal story — Your big "WHY"

This is your deep, personal, sometimes uncomfortable story of why you've dedicated your life servicing people in your industry.

When I say a <u>deep personal</u> *"WHY"*, I mean you must convey to prospects the most emotional things in your life that pushed you into being the professional that you are.

You can no longer be in the transactional business. In you're just taking orders and delivering product, that isn't what the affluent look for. Don't try to play it safe and give a story that makes you comfortable.

Your big *"WHY"* can't be something you feel totally comfortable telling a stranger on the street, such as, *"I value health because I've always been a healthy responsible person."*

That's a very positive, unemotional, and safe reason. That is bad!

> When I was 14 and found food stamps on my mother's kitchen table *(this is when foods stamps were in booklets and not plastic cards)*, I was ashamed that we were so poor.
>
> I thought food stamps were for those poor kids who lived in Albany housing projects 4 blocks down the street from our Brooklyn row house.
>
> That's the day I realized that I was just as poor and I needed to find away above it. This is why I'm in business for myself. To control how much money I earn so I never need to accept a government hand-out.

Now, that's a bit of my personal story.

You need to connect emotionally with your prospect. If you want affluent people to trust you, then **you need to first connect with them emotionally.**

If you said...

"My parents divorced when I was 10. My father all but admitted he found a younger and sexier women he would rather be with. He just wasn't physically attracted to my mom anymore. I became a medical professional to help men and women save their marriages from boredom. It's amazing how a more youthful looking face and body can inject new excitement into a marriage or give someone the confidence to start a new one."

That's a good, big reason *"why"*. It's emotional.

I just made that story up, but can you see how that story would connect with someone emotionally who wanted to hire a cosmetic surgeon?

Your personal story might contain elements that resonate with your potential customer.

> Your personal story is used in the remaining 4 techniques for attracting affluent customers. So take it seriously.
>
> If you play it safe and create an unemotional story, you'll find it very difficult to attract and maintain affluent customers.

Your story must have uncomfortable elements to it to connect with people emotionally. Even if your prospect doesn't connect with your personal story -- the fact that you opened up emotionally helps your prospect trust you because you trusted them enough tell your story.

Your best customers are men over 50 and women over 40.

I'm going to talk more about these two groups to help you find them. I'm spending a lot of time on developing your big *"WHY"* because a poorly crafted one will cripple your success with the affluent.

- Who influenced your beliefs about life and the business you started?

- What moment of truth shaped your philosophy about your industry?

First, the affluent want an emotional connection with you. This creates trust instantly. Then, they want to know about your technical qualifications.

- Why are you so passionate about serving your customers? It can't be just so they can make you rich.

- Why are you the best person to understand their concerns?

- What makes you more than just another "doctor", "roofer", "hair stylist", "personal trainer", etc?

Most elite professionals have powerful personal stories. They have a biography that reflects, in an intimate way, the emotional and social circumstances of their career choice and the unique motivations that promoted a career in their field.

New Economy Rule #2:
Target Men Over 50 & Women Over 40 Years Old

This is the sweet spot for finding people with money who will eagerly pay what you want.

Mark Penn wrote a book entitled, "**Microtrends**". In this book he details the rise of the 'Cougars', affluent women over 40 who want to date younger men. He also makes mention of Men over 50 who want to date younger women.

Even if what you sell have nothing to do with beauty, the fact is that women over 40 and men over 50 have lots of money to spend and they like to spend money.

If you know many affluent people, you'll notice a natural instinct for them to leverage their success and money into youth, sex, longevity, even immortality.

You should start exploiting these facts and target your marketing towards this demographic. It's not enough to just send a brochure in the mail. That's not how you do it.

In the **"Direct Mail"** section of this guide, I'll show you the smart way to use direct mail to attract affluent customers.

New Economy Rule #3:
Clear The Confusion Going On In The Heads Of Potential Customers

Your prospects are often confused about what you sell. It might seem simple to you, but to prospects, they're not sure if they're making a smart decision.

This is why you want to become their trusted advisor. Educate them about what you offer more than trying to sell them on your product or service.

Try to get a deeper understanding about why they want what you sell. Try to find ways to customize their purchase. Offer alternatives of a lower price if that makes more sense, but also offer additional products or services if that is also best for them.

In this New Economy, *you must distinguish yourself* from providers in your industry and those outside your industry. If you don't, you'll end up competing on price -- and competing on price is not how you grow profits. Competing on price puts your business in a race to the bottom.

You end up working more hours, for less money. Those hours at the office take away precious time you could spend with family and friends. Ultimately, this causes you to resent what you do.

Potential customers want you to first educate than about the positives and negatives of various products or services you offer. Consumers will pay more money to the professional who takes the time to educate them first.

You don't want to do this one-on-one. That takes too much time. You need to leverage your time. There are media you can use to help prospects clear the confusion in their heads about the advantages and disadvantages of the various products or services you offer.

- Offer a PDF special report as a download from your website

- Hold an online video seminar: Goto Meeting or Google hangout *(a favorite of my clients)*

- Mail a DVD of a pre-recorded online seminar to people who request it.

- Post a pre-recorded video on your website answering various questions.

You need to start leveraging different forms of media to help prospects clear the confusion in their heads regarding which products or services are best for them.

New Economy Rule #4:
Use Direct Mail In A Smart Way

The wrong way to use direct mail is to send a brochure to a list of people. If you've done that before, you know it's a failed strategy.

How to be smart about direct mail...

I know you may have a sour taste in your mouth regarding direct mail. Some list broker most likely convinced you to *mail 10,000 expensive brochures* to a list he sold you.

But, the mailing flopped big time.

The problem isn't that direct mail stinks. Direct mail works great **if** you get three stars in alignment:

- The right message

- The right prospects

- The right delivery method

The **right message** isn't how many years you've been in business or that you received your degree from an Ivy League school or that you have 5 certifications. No one cares about that because they expect you to have expertise and certifications.

The right message is:

- *Look Great Naked In The Next 6 Weeks:* Weight loss professional

- *New Kitchen, New Bathroom...New Higher Home Value*: Home renovation professional

- *Confused About Your Legal Options When You Can't Pay Your Bills?:* Legal Professional

- Buy 3, Get The 4th Tire, Free: Auto repair professional

The **right prospect** is not anyone from the age of 18-68 who will pay you. You want a list of NYC residents that have purchased a similar product or service that you sell in the last 3-months.

In the case of medical, legal, or financial services, you're looking for a life situation that lends itself to the services you offer.

If you're a cosmetic surgeon, you might target divorced women over 40 with at least 2 kids. If you're an attorney, you might target homeowners that have missed two mortgage payments in a row. If you're a financial planner, you might target new moms because they may want to start college financial planning .

The **right delivery** method isn't a brochure stuffed inside of a #10 size envelope. Do what I do for my cosmetic surgeon clients. Create a kit called...

"Clear The Confusion: 5 Things You Need To Know About Anti-Aging Procedures That Most Professionals Are Too Afraid Tell You!"

This kit should include a...

- Report

- DVD

- Testimonials

- Newsletter

- Certificate to an event or consultation session.

The **report and DVD** answers questions about surgery versus minimally-invasive options for looking years younger or losing weight.

The **Testimonial sheet** or booklet contains words from your satisfied patients. A video testimonial DVD is more powerful.

The **newsletter** demonstrates your knowledge in the anti-aging and weight-loss fields.

Finally, the **certificate** offers the prospect an opportunity to consult with you to better understand their options. Holding an event or seminar where you answer questions is even more powerful.

You can create the same credibility type package for your business. This will help you connect with affluent prospects.

New Economy Rule #5:
The BIGGEST SECRET Of ALL
You Need A Sophisticated "Follow-up" System

You can do everything else correctly --

... *develop your big "why"*

... *target women over 40 and men over 50*

... *clear the confusion in their heads by educating them*

... *use smart direct mail strategies to reach the best prospects*

But, if your follow up system is primitive *(like the one below)*, your results will be poor.

A primitive follow up system...

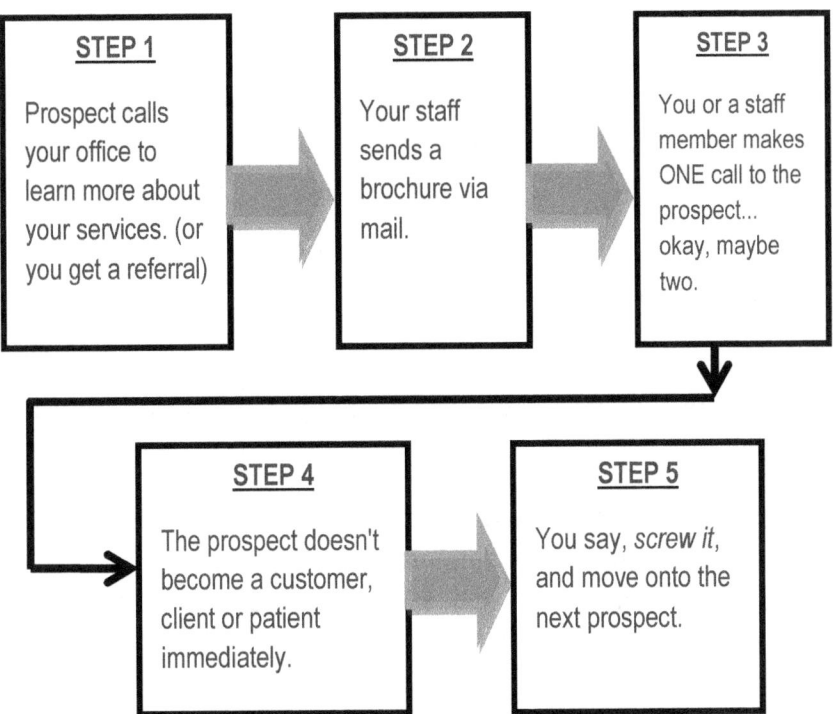

If your follow up system looks something like what's described above, you'll have a very difficult time attracting more affluent people than you can handle. Affluent people expect you to work harder to get them as customers.

YOU NEED A SOPHISTICATED FOLLOW-UP SYSTEM LIKE THIS ONE

If you want to separate yourself from your competitors, your follow up system will need some steroids. You need to drip, drip, drip on your prospects over a 6-month period.

Very few people decide they need something one afternoon, and then call the first website they see online, unless it's plumbing emergency.

You need to develop what I call a C.I.C.F *(Customer Incubator Conversion Funnel)*.

This funnel should use various media types to show affluent prospects that you're competent, in demand by others, and caring.

The affluent don't easily hand over their business to just anyone. However, once you get them as a customer, as long as you don't ignore them, they will come back to you for many more products and services.

What you need is a sophisticated follow up system that most of your competitors are too lazy to implement. Their laziness can be your victory.

Your follow-up system should look something like this...

A SOPHISTICATED FOLLOW-UP SYSTEM THAT ATTRACTS AFFLUENT PATIENTS

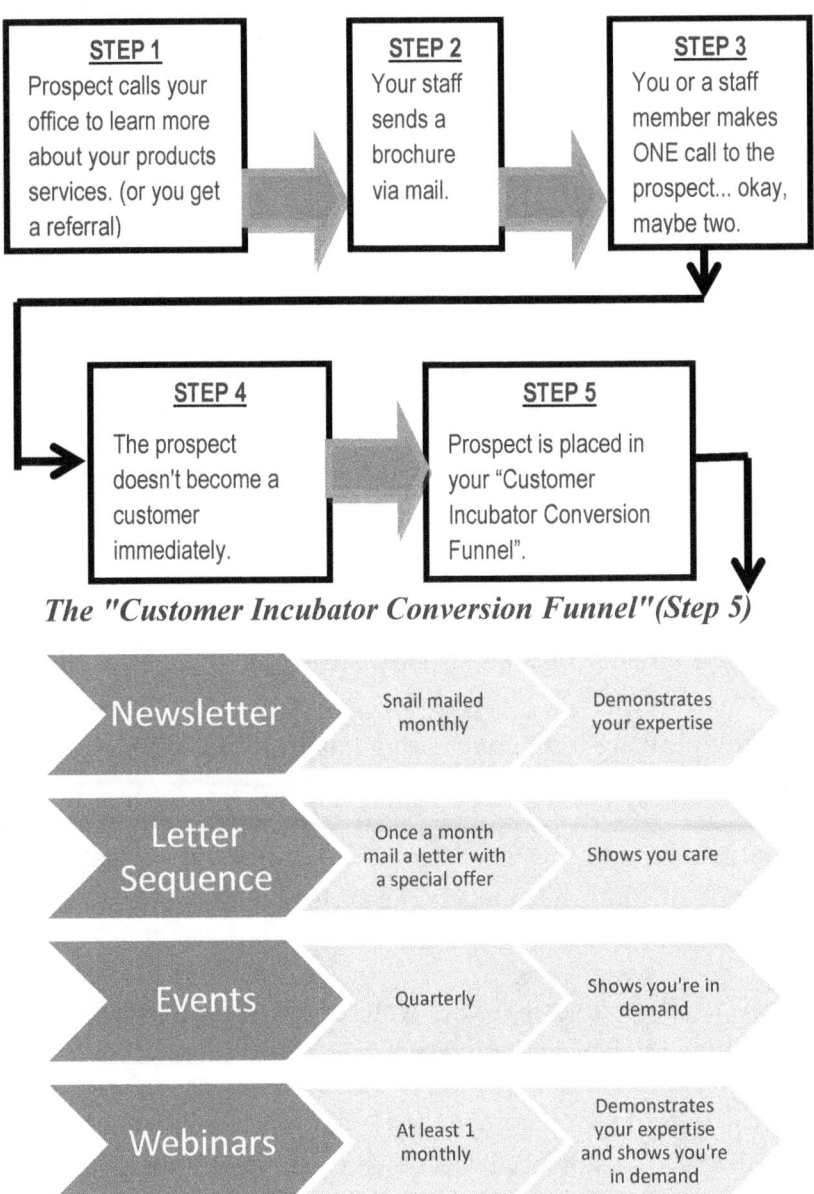

STEP 1
Prospect calls your office to learn more about your products services. (or you get a referral)

STEP 2
Your staff sends a brochure via mail.

STEP 3
You or a staff member makes ONE call to the prospect... okay, maybe two.

STEP 4
The prospect doesn't become a customer immediately.

STEP 5
Prospect is placed in your "Customer Incubator Conversion Funnel".

The "Customer Incubator Conversion Funnel"(Step 5)

Newsletter — Snail mailed monthly — Demonstrates your expertise

Letter Sequence — Once a month mail a letter with a special offer — Shows you care

Events — Quarterly — Shows you're in demand

Webinars — At least 1 monthly — Demonstrates your expertise and shows you're in demand

Your prospects need to soften in your incubator for 3-12 months before you give up on them. I can assure you that most of your competition isn't doing this.

THE LEVELS OF INTEREST YOUR AFFLUENT PROSPECTS WILL SHOW YOU

Affluent prospects have different levels of interest when they contact you for more details about your products or services.

1. Ready Now (5% of prospects)

Every business owner dreams of finding the **"Ready Now"** prospect. These prospects have already decided they want what you sell.

They've done their research. They know which product or service is best for themselves. The **"Ready Now"** prospect is the smallest group of prospects.

Usually, around 5% of prospects are ready to make a buying desision "NOW". They're the easiest to convert, but you can't build a growing business catering only to those who are ready now.

The reason most owners like the **"Ready Now"** prospect is because you don't need much of a systematic follow-up process to convert them to buyers.

They call, you call back, you make initial consultation appointment, they agree to be your next customer -- done deal.

You'll have lots of competition relying on converting these prospects to customers because your competition will follow-up at least once. If your competitor gets to the prospect before you, then you lose.

Top professionals don't expect to build their business or practice on the hopes of meeting the **"Ready Now"** prospect. Only ordinary professionals depend on this class of prospect.

2. Very Interested (5% of prospects)

The **"Very Interested"** prospect is the next best prospect to find.

They require a bit more follow-up. If your follow-up system includes more than just one call or mailed brochure, you have a good chance of converting the **"Very Interested"** prospect to a customer.

Unfortunately, this group is only about 5% of the prospects you'll find.

3. Low Interest (85% of prospects)

This is the **largest group of prospects** you'll encounter and this is where all the money sits and waits.

This represents a huge opportunity for you to transform your business. But, you'll need a very robust, systematic follow-up process like my *"Customer Incubator Conversion Funnel"*.

A robust follow-up system lasts for about 3-months and includes about 30 contacts using email, print, audio, and video formats.

This relentless follow-up pushes the **"Low Interest"** prospect into the **"Very Interested"** group, and then eventually into a **"Ready Now"** prospect.

4. Doesn't Really Care At All (5% of prospects)

If you target your prospects correctly, this group should never be an issue.

Where you advertise, where you network, where you write articles and conduct webinar, determines if you'll attract prospects interested in what you sell.

In this group you'll usually find your competitors and tire kickers responding to your marketing. These people are just curious about what you're up to.

Putting It All Together

What do you think your business would look like if you incorporated all the strategies I discussed with you in this guide?

Do you want to find out?

For existing clients that qualify, we can put this entire system together for your business.

Here's how...

Apply To Join Our Client-Family

GROW YOUR INCOME IN THE NEXT 12-MONTHS
MORE THAN YOU HAVE OVER THE LAST 12-YEARS

As I told you earlier, In this New Economy, you don't want just any type of customer. You want more "dream" customers...*(more affluent customers)*...to make your business recession-proof.

A few new slots have opened in my digital marketing consulting practice for successful NYC businesses who want to double (or triple) their business in The next 12-months

Unfortunately for them *(but fortunate for you)*... I had to let a few clients go who were not as motivated to transform their businesses as I initially thought.

I'm looking for a few "dream" NYC business clients to fill these slots so that I can bring the owners massive windfalls... and **more free time outside the office.**

If you're that client, **I'll personally work with you one-on-one** in your business or practice to help you...

- get more affluent customers who will pay you higher prices and fees

- double or triple your revenue in the next 12 months

- make your competition irrelevant in the minds of prospects

You Pay Nothing Out Of Pocket, Ever

Here's why...

The first thing I'm going to do is personally help you create a strategic plan to attract more high-paying customers.

There's no charge for this and it only takes about 30-45 minutes for us to do together. Yes, we must work together on the initial plan... *(After doing this type of thing since 2010, I've gotten pretty good at fast results).*

I'll even do most of the heavy lifting for you. I'll tell you exactly what to send, how to position your offer...and how to bring in back-end profits from additional services.

At the end of this initial planning session, one of two things will happen:

1. **You'll love the plan and decide to implement it on your own.** If this is the case, I'll wish you the best of

luck and ask that you keep in touch with me to let me know how you're doing.

2. **You'll love the plan and ask to become my client** so I can personally help you execute, maximize, and profit from it ASAP.

If that's the case, we'll knock it out of the park ...**And that's a promise.** Every single one of my clients gets results. Literally. Every. Single. One.

<u>*It's really that simple and there's no catch.*</u>

Think about this.

The "worst" that can happen is you waste 30-45 minutes of your time. The best that can happen is **we work together <u>one-on-one</u>** to generate new affluent customers, clients, or patients for your practice. It's time affluent people start considering your business to spend their money with.

I want to develop a plan to make that a reality.

Transform Your NYC Business
...for FREE!

Here's how it works...

First, we get on the phone, one on one, and go over your business. Although, I'm here in Clinton Hill, Brooklyn, I don't travel to prospects just to chat.

I take a look at what you've got, what you're doing *(and not doing),* and what you want to achieve in the next 12-months.

Once we have those "raw materials", I help you come up with a strategic plan of action to **transform your practice to attract more affluent customers.** In case you're wondering, there are a number of ways I might do this for you. For example, I might show you how to

...**reposition your business** to distinguish your business from competitors who offer deep discounts.

...**target affluent customer** based on *'Affinity Marketing'* principles which help you easily form an emotional bond with prospects to build trust quickly. *(The affluent must trust you before they hire you.)*

...**pull in affluent customers** from untapped sources such as Facebook and Google PPC -- *(Your competition doesn't know how powerful this can be when done the way I do it. This has nothing to do with SEO).*

And like I said, there's *no charge* for this.

Why Would I Make You Such An INSANE OFFER?

Two reasons: **First of all,** I enjoy it...

This type of thing is what I do best. It makes me very happy to see my expertise help a business transform into a medical practice with more affluent customers than they can handle.

Second of all, it's how I attract top-level clients to my inner-circle...

I love the science of selling without really selling. That's what I'm doing right now with you. It's how I want to transform your business to help you attract more affluent customers.

Here's how it works...

Assuming you're happy and you want me to crank out these types of plans for you all the time...you'll probably want us to continue working together long term so I can help you with implementation.

You might be wondering what all of this is going to cost, right?

Well, it's not cheap, however...

If you think about it...**it really doesn't "cost" you anything**.

Let me explain...

I expect to **make you much more than $9,750 in the first month**...and if we keep working together over the next 12 months. I'm confident I can double your entire business ...at minimum.

And look. If you don't want to become a client, don't worry about it. You won't get any sales pitch or pressure from me of any kind -- Ever.

Affluent customers, clients and patients are fun to work with.

They complain less.

They follow your recommendations.

They're not focused on fees, and you can charge them more for superior service.

They actually expect to pay you more!

Best of all, **they make your business recession-proof in this "New Economy"**.

But, consider this...

THIS IS NOT FOR EVERYBODY AND, THIS MAY NOT BE RIGHT FOR YOU

I'm VERY picky about who I'll speak with and I've got a strict *(but reasonable)* set of criteria that needs to be met in order for us to proceed. Here it is:

1. **You have to have a solid business already.**

    This offer is for NYC businesses who are up and running already and simply want to run a lot faster and a lot farther. You should be doing around *$750k to seven figures or more each year* already...with a burning hunger for more.

2. **You must have a steady flow of leads and customers.**

    This means that you're getting consistent prospect flow and converting them into customers already. You're running ads, you're promoting, and you're hungry to test new media to attract new high networth customers.

    If you get 95% of your business from a referral network and you can't imagine spending money to test new media...you don't qualify. You don't have to be "everywhere" or "huge" ...I just need you to be PRESENT in your market.

3. **You must have a prospect list.**

   It doesn't really need to be that big, just responsive. *(In this case: Size actually doesn't matter!)*

4. **You must have a good reputation, and superior service that customers brag about.**

   Everything we do together will not only bring you more affluent customers, but we'll be doing it in a way that creates MASSIVE goodwill in the NYC market.

   In order for us to do that, you need to have your act together with no scandals, legal actions, or pending disputes in the air. *(We have enough of that infecting the political environment in Washington!)*

5. **You MUST follow directions. (Don't worry, I won't ask you to do anything weird or kinky.)**

   After all, if you don't actually implement the stuff I give you, neither one of us will make money.

That's it! Those are all my requirements.

HERE'S WHAT I WANT YOU TO DO NEXT

If you meet the criteria above and would like to talk about developing a blueprint to get you incredible results... then I'll happily set aside some time for you. However...

Due to the intense, one-on-one personalized nature of my consulting practice, I can only work with a handful of new clients. *If you wait too long to contact me, I'll place you on my waiting list in case a spot opens in the future.*

Here's how the process works...

First, you'll need to fill in out an application. Don't worry. It's simple and unobtrusive. I just need to know some details about your business, and to get an idea of what you want to accomplish in the next 12-months.

Second, it takes me about 5 business days to review your application and decide if I can help you -- (and to determine whether or not your business meets my qualifications)

HERE'S WHAT WILL HAPPEN AFTER THAT...

Pat or Stacy from my office will email you to set up a time for us to talk. We use email to set things up to avoid the dreaded "phone-tag" merry-go-round.

Pat and Stacy have been my right- and left-hands since 2010...and are my ONLY employees. One of them will contact you in the next 4 business days at the most.

Our initial call will be between 30 and 45 minutes.

This is where we really begin figuring out exactly what you want ...and how to make it happen.

I'll painstakingly review your goals, positioning with prospects, and so forth ...and I'll deliver a plan to bring in more affluent patients for you.

If you see value in becoming a high level client, great!

We can talk about it.

If you don't want to become a client - that's OK too. No biggie.

WARNING - TIME IS A FACTOR

This opportunity is extremely limited because of the intense one-on-one time needed to provide you with results. Therefore, it's physically impossible for me to work with more than a handful of people.

Once I reach my capacity, I will accept no more clients...period.

I enjoy my free time outside the office.

Also, you should realize there's a very large demand for personal one-on-one help from me -- *and what I'm offering to you is unprecedented* -- and a bit insane.

So with that said, know that the window of opportunity won't be open long.

If you feel like this is right for you, go to **http://chrissewelldigitalmedia.nyc/discoverynyc/** and fill out the application and let's talk.

Talk soon,

Chris Sewell

ABOUT CHRIS SEWELL

How I went from Software Test Engineer with a Top-Secret Security Clearance to lead-generation, marketing strategist to businesses that gross over $1MM a year is a long story. Here, I'll give you the short story.

Born in Brooklyn Jewish hospital *(now called Kingsbrook Jewish Medical Center),* to Carribean parents -- my mother came up with my first name 'Christopher' while riding on the '1' train in Manhattan and passing by 'Christopher Street' Sheridan Square. She was just sitting there on the train, 7-months pregnant with me, the doors open, she say 'Christopher Street' on the tiled walls and decided that would be my name.

She got my middle name 'Jay' from a Jewish co-worker at the old A&S (Abraham & Strauss, now Macys) department store in downtown Brooklyn, where she worked as a cosmetologist since 1974.

Do you find it coincedential that a Black man born in a Jewish hospital, gets a Jewish middle name from a Jewish lady? Maybe there's a little Sammy Davis Jr. in me. Sammy was a Jewish-Black man who performed shows in Vegas with Frank Sinatra back in the 1970s in case you didn't know.

Politically, I feel half Republican, half Democrat. I vote Republican for Mayors and Governors, but Democrat for Presidents, Senators and Congressmen.

I always thought I'd be a Fireman or Police Officer as a kid going to PS 255 elementary school in the Madison section of Brooklyn. I actually had a high opinion of Police officers back then. Not so much today if you've been following the news lately.

When I went to Marine Park junior high in Marine Park Section of Brooklyn, PS 278, I started reading books about being a computer programmer given to me by my mother. I don't think she was too impressed with my Firemen/Policemen dreams when I was 10.

Once I got to Edward R Murrow high school in the Midwood section of Brooklyn, I knew I was pretty damn good with math and science. I decided to become an Electrical Engineer after speaking with my Physics teacher.

I was the only black student in my Physics class. A matter of fact, I was one of maybe three black students in my Algebra. Advanced Algebra, Trigonometry and Advanced Chemistry classes.

At the end of the school day, I would ride the 'M' to the '3' or '4' train back to Crown Heights Brooklyn. This was the 80s when Crown Heights was a war zone. Think the movie 'New Jack City' with Wesley Snipes. Anyway...

I then went to Hostra University for one year and then transferred to the University of Virginia to eventually get my Bachelor and Master degrees in Electrical Engineering. I had a blast at UVA--drinking, partying, smoking weed, women, ah yes, the women --all that college crazy fun. Oh, I did my classwork too. I don't know how, but it got done and I graduated twice.

My first job out of college was at General Electric were I received my Top Secret Security Clearance working on stuff I can't tell you about, otherwise I go the jail for 40 years. I really hated the work I did there, but the money was great!

Eventually, I self studied marketing & advertising from Dan Kennedy, Joe Polish and others. I got damn good at it and began helping friends market their business on the Internet. I realized I needed to charge for my experise and found that businesses really needed the help.

I started Chris Sewell Digital Media to focus on using the Internet and direct mail to generate leads and customers for business owners.

So that's the short story of how I'm here today.

So what's your story?

I'd love to hear it if you qualify to be part of my client family.

http://chrissewelldigitalmedia.nyc/nycdiscovery/

www.ingramcontent.com/pod-product-compliance
Lightning Source LLC
Chambersburg PA
CBHW061223180526
45170CB00003B/1124